A Cast Iron Journey

James P Anderson

Disclaimer

Although the author and publisher have made every effort to ensure that the information in this book was correct at press time, the author and publisher do not assume and hereby disclaim any liability to any party for any loss, damage, or disruption caused by errors or omissions, whether such errors or omissions result from negligence, accident, or any other cause.

Contents

Buying Cast Iron	5
Identifying CI Brands	17
Griswold	21
Wagner	29
Lodge	35
Unmarked CI	43
Unmarked Griswold	47
Unmarked Wagner	51
Unmarked Lodge	53
Unmarked Vollrath	57
Other CI Cookware	63
Birmingham Stove and Range	69
Cleaning Cast Iron	79
Oven cleaner Method	83
Removing Rust	87
Lye Tank	91
Electrolysis Tank	95
Seasoning Cast Iron	103
Cooking and Care	109
Final Thoughts	119
Glossary	123
Appendix	125

Forward

Hello! My name is Jim and I'm a cast-ironaholic! My love for cast iron started after my Dad passed away and I was cleaning out his hunting and camping stuff for my mom. I came across a cast iron pot that was all rusty and had old food still caked on it. Seeing it brought back some wonderful memories of the times Dad and I shared on our hunting and fishing trips. I remember Dad filling up the pot with potatoes, carrots, onions, some kind of meat and spices, then burying it in the coals before we headed out for the day's hunt. We'd come back after dark and scoop the insides of the pot because the edges were a bit crisp. Boy, it sure was good and great memories were made.

Well, to honor those memories, and my Dad, I decided I was going to clean it up and use it. I did some research and found a way to strip it clean and season it. It took me quite a while to get it cleaned so I could season it, but eventually, I got there. After I seasoned it up, I was blown away at how good it looked, and I was hooked! So, I asked my wife where her cast iron skillets were that she had before we were married. After restoring those, there was no turning back. I went on a cast iron finding and buying spree. I couldn't get enough! All I wanted to do was find a really cool piece and restore it. What am I saying, I wanted to restore any and all cast iron I could get my hands on! As time has gone on in my love of cast iron, I have become a little more selective in my purchases.

I decided to write this book to help others who have just found the cast iron world and need a little guidance on their first steps to obtaining a quality piece of cast iron. Whether you are just looking for a piece to cook with or you want to start collecting, I hope there is a little info in here for everyone.

I want to thank my wife (Sue) and my kids (Mitchell and Valerie) for putting up with my cast iron obsession. I know it can be overbearing at times, but if you just stick with me a little longer, I'm sure it will turn out all right. LOL. I'm so happy I found the world of cast iron. I couldn't imagine cooking on anything else ever again!

Thanks for allowing me to share my thoughts and happy collecting,

Jim Anderson

Introduction

In this book, we will discuss the searching, buying, cleaning, and seasoning of cast iron (CI) cookware. There will also be a small section on cooking with cast iron. I will not, however, be talking about the value of collectible CI. The value of cast iron is only that which the buyer feels comfortable paying. Remember, cast iron is for life if treated with respect.

Quality care of your iron will make it an heirloom to hand down for generations to come. Some of my favorite skillets to use are a hundred years old and look like they just came off the showroom shelf. I will go through the stripping processes that I have found to be the easiest, safest (for you and your CI), and most cost-effective for you. Likewise, we will talk about my seasoning process and others that are out there.

There is no right way or wrong way to clean and care for your CI, but there are ways to make it safer and easier. The techniques discussed in this book are solely mine. They are what I believe to be the best way. Our ancestors had their ways and they worked, but there are new ways that are more efficient.

So, with that in mind, I will not be talking about using fire, self-cleaning ovens or power tools to clean cast iron. In my opinion, these methods increase the chance of damaging a skillet that could be a family heirloom or a very valuable piece. Instead, we will talk about using lye and electrolysis for the stripping of cast iron. We will also talk about different oil and temps to season your CI.

I'm sure there will be a lot of people out there that won't agree with everything I've outlined in this book, but for the novice collector or user, this book should at least help to get you started on your journey into the world of cast iron!

I hope you enjoy the book!

Buttermilk Biscuits With Sausage and Gravy

Biscuits

3 cups all-purpose flour
2 tablespoons sugar
2 1/2 teaspoons baking powder
1/2 teaspoon baking soda
1/2 teaspoon salt
1/2 cup lard
1 1/4 cups buttermilk
1/4 cup butter, melted and divided

Sausage Gravy

1 pound Breakfast Sausage
3/4 cup flour
4 1/2 cups milk
1/2 tablespoon freshly cracked black pepper
Salt to taste
2 tablespoons butter

Preheat oven to 450°F. In large bowl mixing bowl, combine flour, sugar, baking powder, baking soda, salt pepper. Cut in lard with a fork until crumbly. Gradually add buttermilk, stirring just until dry ingredients are moistened. Dough should be sticky. Do not overwork dough.

On a lightly floured surface, roll dough to 1/2-inch thickness with floured rolling pin. Cut 12 biscuits with a 2 1/2-inch round biscuit cutter. Place biscuits in cast iron skillet that has been greased, and brush tops with half of melted butter. Bake for 12 to 14 minutes, or until lightly browned. Brush with remaining melted butter before serving.

While biscuits are baking, start gravy. In large cast iron skillet, cook sausage over medium-high heat until browned and crumbly. Reduce heat to medium and add flour to sausage; mix thoroughly. Cook until flour browns, about 4 minutes stirring constantly.
Add milk slowly and increase heat to medium-high. Continue to stir. Add pepper and salt. As the gravy comes to a boil, it will thicken. If too thick, add additional milk. After boiling, reduce heat to a simmer and add butter

Buying Cast Iron

Where do I buy cast iron? How do I know if it's a good buy? These are typical questions of a person who is new to cast iron. The answers can be as different as the people you're buying them from.

I've never seen a bad piece of cast iron unless it's cracked or broken. Even a cracked piece can still be used for baking and cooking sometimes. Whether it's American made or foreign made, cast iron acts relatively the same way. Some cast iron is very collectible, and collectors are searching high and low for that special piece. Other people are just looking for a skillet to cook with. No matter which category you fall in, there's a piece out there for you. I've found that searching for cast iron can be a fun adventure. Talking and trading stories with people is fun and can be very informative. A lot of the time, you're looking at a skillet that has been in their family for generations. Just think of the stories those skillets could tell!

I've found CI in antique stores, thrift stores, flea markets, second-hand stores, restaurants, and garage sales. I've even found one sticking out of a snow bank! Wherever you find it, you'll need to know if it's worth buying. Starting with your eyes is the best way. Look the piece over, top to bottom, front to back, and side to side for cracks and chips. Sometimes it's hard to tell because there's so much build up or rust you just can't tell. That's when you'll have to make your own judgment and determine if the price is right for you. Remember, you're going to have it for a lifetime, so the price is kind of irrelevant. What's a skillet you'll have for a lifetime worth? A dollar a year for the time you have it and use it? You'll also want to see if it sits flat. This can be done by placing on a piece of flat glass or floor. I carry a straight edge with me when I'm picking. Some skillets are bowed up or down. If bowed down it could be what's called a spinner.

While you're trying to decide what brand or style of cast iron to buy, keep in mind that the most collectible skillet won't necessarily outcook a non-collectible skillet of any make. Different foundries cast their iron in different ways. Some skillets are thicker and heavier, while others are thinner and lighter. This is good to keep in mind if weight is an issue for you. I have found that the older the skillet is, the lighter it seems to be compared to its more modern counterpart. Newer skillets for sale in chain stores are already pre-seasoned and heavier but can be used right out of the box.

I have found the best places to find cheap, but good quality CI is at garage sales. These skillets have usually been treated better and taken care of with love. I hit somewhere around 200 garage sales a year and only find CI at maybe 1 in 60 stops. Never be afraid to ask people at garage sales if they have cast iron for sale. They may not even realize people would want to buy it. Thrift stores, such as Goodwill and Salvation Army, have produced some excellent skillets that are reasonably priced. When you go to the antique stores, just remember, they are trying to stay in business and have their prices marked accordingly. Don't get me wrong, I've found some really good deals at antique stores, but they are few and far between.

Let's assume that you are looking for a skillet to just cook in. What size do you think you'll need? The size of the skillet you'll need will depend on what you're making. You obviously can't cook a whole chicken in a #3 one egg skillet. It just wouldn't fit. For the person who isn't looking for a whole set, I would recommend a #8 skillet. It's a fairly large size skillet, most are between 10" and 10 ½" across, but still small enough to handle. A small set of skillets, a #3, a #5 and #8 should be able to handle most any meal you make.

There are also many online places to buy cast iron. Ebay, Craigslist, Etsy, and Facebook sites are some

of them. All I will say about them is, do your research on the seller and be careful of scams. Asking for pictures of the piece that isn't already shown is a good way to make sure they are actually in possession of it. I'm not trying to scare you from buying from these sites. I'm just letting you know that there are scammers out there selling CI. Personally, I find the cast iron for sale groups on Facebook to be more reputable. Always find out how the piece will be packed when buying on these sites. Remember, it has to go through the mail, FedEx, or UPS, and we all know how careful they are with our packages!
I also recommend using PayPal when purchasing online.

The condition of the piece you are looking at can be anywhere from totally covered in rust or gunk to already clean and ready for use. Either way, I'll show you how to make it look new and be useable.

When looking at a piece that's rusted, you'll want to be sure of a few things. First, is it really rust, or could it be fire damage? Some people will use fire to clean their CI (NOT RECOMMENDED). They do this by throwing a skillet into the coals of a very hot fire and pulling it out when the coals die down. This process will take your skillet down to bare metal for sure, but with the amount of heat generated by the fire, warping can occur. Sometimes, when CI gets really hot, it changes the molecular structure of the metal and the piece won't hold the seasoning as well or at all. If you've determined that it is just rust, you'll want to look at the cooking surface and see if the rust has pitted it. The pitting doesn't mean that you can't use it, it's just going to take cooking time to fill in the pits and make it smooth.

Sometimes, you'll find a skillet that will have little marks on the cooking surface. This is fine. It's just the tool marks from years of cooking great meals. Some skillets will have what appears to be grind marks on the lip of the skillet. These are where the cast was poured at the foundry and was then ground smooth. This is normal and won't affect your cooking or the value of the skillet. No matter what the condition you find a skillet in, it can almost always be made to be useable again.

Having a few tools out in the field with you will help with determining the quality of the piece you are considering. Some of the tools that are helpful while out in the field looking for cast iron are a tape measure, straight edge, magnet (CI is magnetic, Aluminum is not), pocket flashlight, pocket knife, and knowledge. Don't let someone take advantage of you because you didn't do a little research first. Some skillet brands have been copied over time. These are usually a different size than the originals. Knock offs can be foreign or American made. Knowing the size in inches and using a tape measure in the field will help.

When you are using your cast iron, it's optimal to have a flat cooking surface and bottom of skillet. When looking to purchase a used skillet, by having a straight edge, such as a small ruler, you can make sure that it's flat. Just lay the straight edge on the bottom of the skillet and on the cooking surface. If any part of the skillet is not touching the ruler, a little warping may have occurred. This does not mean that it's not a purchasable piece, just that it's not completely flat. When cooking over a fire or on a gas stove, this may not be a problem at all. When cooking on a glass top stove, if it is bowed out towards the bottom, it will spin like a top. It is still useable but will spin rather easily. If the bottom is bowed up, you will have a skillet where all the liquid will go towards the edges.

Some cast iron is chrome or nickel plated and at times looks like aluminum. I've had many people ask me about cookware that they think is cast iron and turns out to be aluminum. Cast aluminum is heavy, but not as heavy as cast iron. Having a magnet in your pocket when picking can alleviate that situation. Remember, steel also is magnetic but is much lighter than cast iron.

A small flashlight and pocket knife can be very valuable to you in your hunt for cast iron. A flashlight will help you seek out little cracks and imperfections that you may not be able to see. If you see what may be a crack, using a pocket knife and carefully scraping across the spot may help you decide whether it is a crack or just built up of seasoning. Remember, it's not your skillet yet, so be careful. Some shop owners may not like you scraping on their merchandise!

Knowledge! I think this is the most important tool to have in your arsenal. They say that knowledge is power, and I truly believe this when picking cast iron. When you go into a store or are at a garage sale, knowing what you are looking at and knowing how much you should be paying is huge. When you find a piece and it's coated with gunk or rust so bad that you can't see any cracks or markings to determine what it is, you're taking a chance. It would be beneficial for you not to spend too much money at this point. You just don't know what you are getting. That doesn't mean it's not a good skillet or even a collector's piece, just that you can't be sure what it is. I have over 300 pieces of CI and other than a few special ones to fill in sets I'm collecting, the average price I've paid for a skillet is $19. There are some really good deals out there, you just have to find them and be willing to walk away when the price is more than what it is worth.

So, with all this in mind, let's go find some cast iron!

Pound Cake

2 sticks butter, extra for greasing the pan, at room temperature
Pinch salt
3 cups sugar
6 large eggs, at room temperature
3 cups sifted all-purpose flour (sifted before measuring)
1 cup heavy cream, refrigerated or at room temperature
Scant tablespoon vanilla extract

Instructions

Preheat the oven to 325 degrees.
Affix the rack in the center position in the oven.
Generously grease the cast iron pan with the extra softened butter.
Beat the butter and salt in a large bowl and beat, medium low speed until it's creamy.
Gradually add the sugar, mixing it in on medium-low speed. Increase speed to medium and beat until pale in color, about 1 minute.
Reduce the speed to medium low and add the eggs, one at a time, beating well after each addition. Scrape down the sides of the bowl as necessary.
One medium low speed start adding the flour, one third at a time. After the first addition, add half the cream, beating it in well. Mix in another third of flour followed by the rest of the cream. On medium low speed add the

vanilla and scrape down the sides of the bowl. Turn the batter into the prepared pan.

Bake until the top is golden brown and crackly, about 65 to 75 minutes. A toothpick inserted should come out clean. Remove the pan to a rack and cool at least 1 hour. When ready to unmold, run a knife around the perimeter of the pan, giving the pan a good shake. Invert the cake onto a cooling rack and invert again to so that the cake rests top side up. Allow to cool for at least another hour before serving. It will store well in a tightly covered cake stand with dome top or wrap in foil for extra long keeping (about 5 days).

Identifying
CI Brands

Identifying cast iron can be easy and it can be hard. Some cast iron foundries put their names on the skillets and others don't. Marked cast iron makes it very easy to figure out what you're looking at, while unmarked cast iron can leave you scratching your head. In this section, I will talk about both marked and unmarked foundries. This will not be a complete list of every foundry that ever was but will give you a general idea of identifying cast iron.

There is a wide range of cast iron cookware available. I will touch on some of the most common brands that are out there. The most collectible cast iron is manufactured in the United States. Companies like Griswold, Wagner, and Lodge are very highly sought-after. Other unmarked skillets tend to get overlooked by collectors and others because they don't have a name on them. Like I stated before, most all cast iron cookware works relatively the same. How they cook will be determined by your knowledge of cooking with cast iron, not the iron itself.

Different characteristics of cast iron cookware can help identify and age skillets. Words like heat ring (inside or outside), milled, grooved, smooth bottom, single notch, three notch, no notch and hammered are terms used to describe different cast iron. Knowing these words and what they mean can help in identification.

Cast iron skillets come with numbers, either raised or incised, on the handles or the bottoms. These numbers are not indicating the size of the skillet, but the size of the eye hole on a coal or wood burning stove it would fit. Collectors use these numbers to keep track of sets.

Griswold

Ok, let's start with the most well-known brand, Griswold. The Holy Grail of cast iron!
The Griswold Manufacturing Co. was in business from 1865 to 1957 and was located in Erie, PA. They are easily recognizable by the "cross" logo that appeared on their products from 1910 through the 1960s. The logo style changed several times during those years, but always with the trademark cross.

For about the first ten years, the cross logo had the name Griswold in it at a slanted angle. The "SLANT LOGO" is very collectible and are usually priced quite high, especially at antique stores and online.

At some point during the 1920s the logo changed to block lettering.

This is probably the most recognizable of all the Griswold logos. This logo is known as the "Large Block Logo" (LBL).

Early in 1940, Griswold changed the logo again. This time they made the logo much smaller and still with the block lettering.

Known as the "Small Block Logo" (SBL) it was used until 1957 when Griswold was bought by the Randall Corp., at which time the foundry was closed in Erie, PA. After the closing, all Griswold cookware was produced by the Wagner Foundry in Sydney, OH.

They were still produced with the Griswold logo from 1957 to 1965 but did not include the "ERIE PA" mark. In the 1960s some of the cookware was made with dual logos, with both Wagner and Griswold.

Griswold had three variations of its handles over the years.

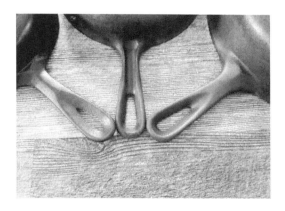

The first style is referred to as the "Early Handle". Used from roughly 1939 to 1944, this has a teardrop-shaped opening on the handle with the point closest to the pan. The underside of the handle has a recessed area that is a tapered teardrop shape but is larger than the opening.

The second style is called the "Grooved Handle. It looks exactly like the late handle from above, but when viewed from below, the whole underside of the handle is grooved out the whole length of it.

The third style is called the "Late Handle". The opening on this handle doesn't have a point on either end. It is rounded on both ends but tapers down smaller on the end near the pan. The underside of the handle still has a recessed area around the opening, but still comes to a point.

Before the cross logo was on the bottom of Griswold cookware, the word "ERIE" graced their pans. Some people believe these to be pre-Griswold. This, however, is not true. Matthew Griswold and the Seldon's were both involved in the production of the "ERIE" skillets at the time. The "ERIE" cast iron skillet was in production from the early 1880s to 1907.

The timeline of the "ERIE" skillets is divided into 6 time periods (or series), which can help collectors determine when a skillet was produced.

There is a logo, that every Griswold collector is always looking for, but very few will ever find. The "SPIDER" logo. Only produced for a short time during the "ERIE" period, this logo is unusual. It has a raised logo in the shape of a skillet bodied spider on a web with the "ERIE" on the spider's back. Since this logo was raised, instead of incised, it wore off quickly with use. This and the fact they were made for such a short time is what makes them extremely collectible and valuable. Most estimates date it only during the early 1890s.

One last thought on Griswold, even though they are the collector's dream, they are not out of touch for the common user. Many can be found at reasonable prices and in good shape. Remember, Griswold made many different types of cookware, such as Waffle Irons, Dutch Ovens, Skillets, Griddles, etc....

Pancakes

1 ½ cups All-Purpose Flour
2 teaspoons of Baking Powder
½ teaspoon Salt
1 tablespoon Sugar
1 Egg, beaten
1 ¼ cup Buttermilk
2 Tablespoons Lard or shortening.

Directions

Slowly heat the griddle for about 15 minutes.
Sift together dry ingredients, Flour, Baking Powder, Salt and Sugar, set aside.
Mix together wet ingredients, Egg, Buttermilk and Lard, set aside.
Test the griddle: Place a few drops of cold water on griddle, if they dance about, griddle is ready.
Stir the wet ingredients into the dry until just slightly dampened. Ignore the lumps.
Pour 1/2 cup of batter onto heated griddle.
When edges of pancakes become dry and some of the bubbles break, turn them.
The second side will cook in about ½ the time it took to cook the first side.
Remove from griddle.
Rub the griddle with the salt bag between making each pancake to clean, if needed.
Add just a little oil to lightly grease the griddle before adding more batter.

Wagner

The Wagner Manufacturing Company started in 1891 and continued to produce cookware until 1952 when it was sold. The new owners continued to make the Wagner brand are still manufacturing the brand today.

The Wagner logo started in the 1890s with the name "WAGNER' and used it for 30 years.

It was either in a straight line or in an arc (1891-1910). In 1895 they added "SIDNEY -O-" underneath it and continued until 1920. The logo was also seen at the 12 o'clock position and the center position during these times.

Somewhere around the 1920s the Wagner logo changed, and the word "WARE" was added. The logo now read "WAGNER WARE SIDNEY -O-".

From this logo, Wagner's most iconic trademark was developed. One large fancy script "W" for both words, with the SIDNEY -O- beneath. This logo also moved around on the skillet bottoms. The "PIE LOGO" appeared in the center of the pan between 1924 and 1934. This logo has the words "WAGNER WARE SIDNEY -O-" inside a pie shape.

Dating a Wagner skillet is a little harder to put to a specific year. Time spans of production on certain styles range 30 years, like 1925-1957. Styles of logo and handles can help narrow it down with some research. Wagner skillets are very collectible, the high quality of casting produced very few flaws and smooth cooking surfaces. Wagner, like Griswold, produced many types of cookware, and this helped bring them to the forefront of the industry. Items such as Dutch Ovens, Griddles,

Gem Pans, Waffle Irons, and skillets are a few of the cookware items they offered.

During the time Wagner was producing their own logo skillets and cookware, retail stores were looking for cookware that was affordable to everyone. Wagner produced many items for companies like Montgomery Wards, Sears and others. These cast iron pieces did not bear the Wagner name. Instead, they had no logo and only the skillet size. They are known as unmarked Wagners. They still hold the quality and craftsmanship for which Wagner was known.

Beef stew

1 boneless beef chuck roast (2 pounds), cut into 1/2-inch cubes
1 tablespoon lard
1 large onion, chopped
5 cups water
1 teaspoon salt
1/2 teaspoon pepper
5 to 6 medium potatoes, peeled and cut into 1/2-inch cubes
5 medium carrots, cut into 1/4-inch slices
1 medium rutabaga, peeled and cut into 1/2-inch cubes
1 cup sliced celery (1/2-inch pieces)
1/2 medium head cabbage, finely sliced
1/4 cup all-purpose flour
3/4 cup cold water
2 teaspoons browning sauce, optional

Directions

In a Dutch oven over medium-high heat, brown meat in oil. Add the onion, water, seasoned salt, pepper and salt if desired; bring to a boil. Reduce heat; cover and simmer for 2 hours.
Add the vegetables; cover and simmer for 30 minutes or until the meat and vegetables are tender. Combine flour, cold water and browning sauce until smooth. Stir into stew. Bring to a boil; cook and stir for 2 minutes or until thickened and bubbly.

Lodge

Lodge Cast Iron was founded by Joseph Lodge in 1896. They are still in business today, making them the longest operating cast iron foundry still operating in the USA. The foundry is located in South Pittsburg, TN. Originally, the foundry was named Blacklock, until it burnt down in 1910. After it was rebuilt, the foundry was renamed Lodge Manufacturing Company. Many collectors would love to find a Blacklock skillet, and some claim to have one, but there is really no way to be absolutely sure. Very few cookware pieces from Blacklock were marked, and with the foundry fire, a lot of records were destroyed. So, I'll start with the known Lodge brand.

Lodge's first skillet is known as a "NO NOTCH" Lodge.

Produced from 1910-1920 this skillet came with or without the "ARC" Lodge logo and the handle came with or without raised numbers. Some skillets didn't even have a number on the back. Late "NO NOTCH" Lodges will have a raised makers mark like the single notch does.

"SINGLE NOTCH": The "NOTCH" refers to a groove in the heat ring at the 12 o'clock position. This Lodge skillet was produced from the late 1920s to 1940. The same characteristics as in the No Notch are found on these skillets. The only difference is the "SINGLE NOTCH" in the heat ring.

"THREE NOTCH": Like the single notch, the three notch had the same notch at the 12 o'clock position, but also had a notch at the 3 o'clock and 9 o'clock positions. When they were first produced in 1940, the 12 o'clock notch was more pronounced than the side notches were. These skillets also had a raised makers mark. This more pronounced notch is due to the fact that the skillets were still being handmade.

There was a period of time that Lodge did not use a logo. This period of time ranges around 1940-1974. They did this to save money on patterns and production. They were marketing their cookware in many outlets and those outlets wanted quality items from a known maker. It was easier and cheaper for them to run one production line during those times. Each age through those times show differences and can help you date them.

1940-1945 gives you a 3 notch with raised makers mark at 6 o'clock position
.

1946-1953 you have a 3 notch with only a number, no other markings (none)

1954-1965 you still have the 3 notch with a number, but also has various pattern marks (incised letters or numbers) on the bottom. They can be located in different areas and in singular or multiples marks. It was a way to track pattern use.

In 1965 Lodge started using prefix and suffix symbols on their skillets. These prefixes and suffixes are letter symbols such as SK, DO, CF, CS, etc.... At this time, Lodge is at full automated molding, meaning that they no longer are made by hand, but on a production line instead. The plain SK is used into the 1980s.

1974 is the introduction of the "Large Egg Logo". These are very easy to identify, and they also carry the prefix/suffix system. They were done at the same time as the SK pieces. During this time, we also see the plain numbered skillets with a blob shift mark. This was probably done as a contract request by the retailer.

Lodge still continues to manufacture cast iron cookware to this day. Even though it's not handmade anymore and is a little heavier than antique cast iron, it is still great cast iron to cook on and is inexpensive.

Unmarked
Cast Iron

As with marked cast iron, unmarked CI can be very collectible. Some pieces fetch amounts equal to some of the higher marked brands. Since there were hundreds of foundries throughout the United States, there happen to be tons of unmarked quality cast iron out there. Most of these foundries left their pieces unmarked because it helped keep the costs down and was more appealing to retailers who could sell at lower prices.

Some of the larger foundries also made unmarked cast iron. They, too, wanted to get in on the sale of cast iron to people who couldn't afford the brand names. Companies like Griswold, Wagner, and Lodge produced these unmarked pieces for many years during the 20th century.

As with marked cast iron, using certain characteristics of unmarked cast iron from known foundries can help you figure out what you are looking at. With that thought in your head, remember, with so many foundries that were ever in business, there's no way to possibly have all the info on each of them. Even the known foundries that produced unmarked CI don't always have the best records on them. So dating some unmarked pieces can be tough or fall in a large time frame.

I'll go through a few of the most sought after and easier to identify unmarked brands that are out there. Just like the marked collector pieces, unmarked CI was sometimes copied. Both are known as Repos and even though they can be good for use, they are not collectible. Some of the other brands out there that no one knows anything about, but the skillets keep turning up have been given names such as Southern Mystery Skillet (SMS).

So, let's go on a trip into unmarked cast iron!

Unmarked Griswold

Griswold "Iron Mountain" series was produced from 1930-1940.

Developed to compete with other brands in chain style stores, it is very easy to identify this skillet.

With a very distinctive style handle and blocky italic font on the bottom with heat ring. These skillets are sought after by some collectors but are overlooked by others that have no clue what they are. They cook and have the quality of Griswold standards.

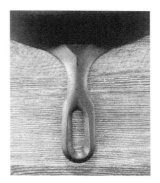 

Griswold made other skillets for retail chain stores. In the 1920s, they produced "Best Made" for Sears, Roebuck & Co. These also have the italic font. There is also a "Good Health" skillet, manufactured in the 1920s-1930 and also has the italic font, with lower case letters. Neither of these two has the distinct handle of the Iron Mountain. There are a couple of others out there as well, Puritan and Merit.

Grandmother Crites Feather Dumplings

2 cups sifted flour
1 tbsp. salt
1 tsp. baking powder
ring fingernail full pepper (1/4 tsp)
pinky fingernail full of sage (1/8 tsp.) "optional"
1 egg, well beaten
3 tbsp. melted butter
roughly 2/3 cup milk

Directions

Sift dry ingredients together. Add egg, melted butter, and enough milk to make a moist, stiff batter. Drop by teaspoons into boiling stock (chicken or beef) in a large cast iron dutch oven. These will get large. Cover very closely and cook for 8 minutes. NO LOOKING!!!
Makes about 2 dozen.

Unmarked Wagner

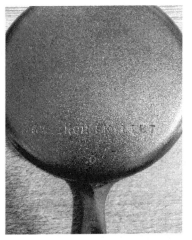

Unmarked Wagner skillets have all the same characteristics that the marked ones do except, obviously, no logo. They do, however, have the skillet size incised on the bottom at 6 o'clock. The font on these pans is a Times New Roman style. Also, they will have an incised number on the handle. Made in the USA was added after 1960 below description.

Wagner also made other store brand skillets such as Long Life and Wardway. These were produced in the 1920s and '30s and have the words on the bottoms.

Unmarked Lodge

In the earlier section on Lodge, I touched on some of the skillets that they made without their logo. These were the "No Notch", "Single Notch" and "3 Notch". Some skillets that are out there are attributed to Lodge because they have the three notches in the heat ring on the bottom.

Biscuit Bread

2 teaspoons of bacon drippings
2 cups of self rising flour
1/4 cup very cold butter, cubed
3/4 to 1 cup cold buttermilk
2 tablespoons of butter, melted, optional

Instructions

In an 8-inch cast iron skillet, melt the bacon fat over medium high heat. Meanwhile, cut the cold butter into the flour. Add only enough buttermilk to the flour to form into a shaggy dough, turn out onto a floured surface, sprinkle a small amount of flour on top and quickly shape into a disc. Turn over, sprinkle additional flour on top and tighten disc, just slightly smaller than the skillet.
Transfer the dough to the hot skillet. Cover and reduce heat to between medium and medium low. Cover and cook until the bread browns on the bottom, then flip over, pour melted butter on top if desired, cover and cook until browned on the other side

Unmarked Vollrath

The Vollrath Company is located in Sheboygan, WI. While they are not known for their cast iron skillets (they manufactured many different products), they are, in my opinion, one of the nicest and lightest skillets out there.

They are recognizable by their outside heat ring (smooth bottom does exist) with a number incised, with or without dashes, at the 3 o'clock position and it's turned sideways to the handle.

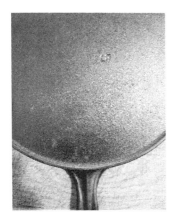

Sideways number to handle

The handle is hollowed out on the bottom and has a long reinforcement rib that runs from pan side to handle hole.

 The top of the handle appears to curve downwards.

The top of the handle has a number incised on it.

Sweet and Sour BBQ Sauce

1 box onion soup mix (both envelopes)
1/2 c. sugar
    1/2 tsp. pepper
    1/4 c. mustard
    2 c. ketchup
    1/4 c. lemon juice
    1c. pickle juice

Directions

Mix all together in a well seasoned cast iron sauce pan and simmer for 10 minutes. If too thick add a little water

Birmingham Stove and Range Unmarked BSR

Birmingham Stove and Range (BSR) was located in Birmingham, AL. They made two series of skillets, the "Red Mountain" and the "Century".

The Red Mountain series was produced from the 1930s-1940s. It can be identified by its handle, its rim and the font on the bottom.

The handle of this skillet is like no other, with a very prominent ridge on the bottom of the handle, it runs from pan to handle hole.
This handle is the same on both series.

The rim of the skillet has no definitive lip or edge. The side of skillet runs smoothly up to the top. The Red Mountain series skillet is lighter and smoother cast than the Century Series.

The Century series skillet was produced from 1954-1957.

It, too, can be identified by its unique handle, font and the addition of "USA" on the bottom.

The size number on the bottom also now has the mark, for example (NO.3) and the pan size in (6 ⅝ IN) and MADE IN USA.

The lip on the Century series is very pronounced and can clearly be seen and felt. The Century is an all-around heavier and more porous cast.

Other CI Cookware

As I have mentioned before, many foundries made cookware items other than skillets. There are many different pieces available that are designed to help in making specialty dishes. From making rolls, breadsticks, cornbread, and waffles, you will find a huge variety of pieces to choose from. Some of these pieces of CI can be very collectible, while others are a dime a dozen. Using some of these pieces can be a bit of a challenge. With all the little intricate designs on the pieces, they can be a bear sometimes to get what you made out. With a good restoration and proper seasoning, this problem shouldn't surface. I'm not going to go into great detail about these pieces of CI, because there are so many out there that this book would be thousands of pages and really boring. Instead, I'm just going to show you some and tell you what they are called.

Waffle Irons (WI). Almost every foundry had a waffle iron in their line up. Waffles have been a breakfast choice for people for a very long time and the cast iron foundries capitalized on that. A well seasoned WI is hard to beat when making waffles.

Chicken Fryer (CF). Chicken fryers were a common sight in kitchens back in the day. Fried chicken wasn't purchased at KFC back then. It was made at home. A chicken fryer is what you used. A deep sided skillet with a lid were the qualities of the chicken fryer.

Dutch Ovens (DO). No kitchen was without a good Dutch oven. When a roast or a stew was to be cooked, the Dutch Oven was used. Baking bread was a breeze in a DO. A versatile, heavy pot with lid.

Griddles. No kitchen is complete without a griddle. Griddles are a versatile piece of cast iron. With low sidewalls, it makes it easy to make pancakes, french toast, grilled cheese, and even tortillas. I've even used mine to make cookies on.

Turks Head Pan. A Turks Head pan is made for making bread or cakes that turn out looking like a Turk's Head knot. A decorative knot containing many interwoven strands.

Muffin Pans. Quite a few muffin pans are available, they were made by many companies. They came in different sizes. This one is an 11 cup.

Gem Pans. A gem pan is a pan that has separate little cavities that are attached together. They were used to make little cakes or pies. The term "Gem" most likely comes from the little cakes that came out looking like gems.

Brown Sugar Syrup

Mix 2 to 1

2 cups dark brown sugar packed
1 cup water
vanilla and butter as you wish

Mix the water and brown sugar over medium heat, bring to a slow boil, stirring and making sure sugar is totally dissolved, reduce heat to a low boil and cook 4-5 minutes, add vanilla and butter after removing from heat

Cleaning Cast Iron

Here's a touchy subject for you. While there are a bunch of different ways to strip cast iron to bare metal for seasoning, I'm going to discuss only the ways that I, personally, have proven to be safe for cast iron. I know, your grandpa just threw it in a fire to clean it. While a technique like that will definitely clean the crud from your skillet, it could warp it or even change the molecular structure of the metal and make it very, very hard for the seasoning to stick.

The methods we'll be talking about are going to clean your skillet and prepare it for seasoning, so it can be used and handed down for generations to come. No matter where your skillet came from, whether it be a family heirloom or a skillet you got at the store yesterday, it will last your lifetime, and others as well, if taken care of properly.

Let's start with this: Exactly what is it we are trying to remove from the skillet? Well, it's usually just built-up crud from all those wonderful years of making meals for someone. Or it could be rusty from years of neglect. Or a combination of both. Whichever it is, we need to remove it.

I practice three ways of removing old crud from my cookware and two for rust. Electrolysis, Lye and

Oven cleaner. All three will remove organic crud from your skillets, while electrolysis and vinegar will remove rust. Let's start with the way I learned when I first started.

Potato Cakes

Ingredients
3 large potatoes (about 2 pounds), peeled
2 large eggs, lightly beaten
1 tablespoon grated onion
2 tablespoons all-purpose flour
1 teaspoon salt
1/2 teaspoon baking powder
Vegetable oil for frying

Directions
Finely grate potatoes. Drain any liquid. Add eggs, onion, flour, salt, and baking powder. In a frying pan, add oil to the depth of 1/8 in.; heat over medium-high (375°). Drop batter by heaping tablespoonfuls in hot oil. Flatten into patties. Fry until golden brown, turning once. Serve immediately.

Oven Cleaner Method

To strip organic material from your cast iron with oven cleaner is fairly easy, but a little time-consuming. This process can be a little dangerous if a small amount of safety is not followed. When working with oven cleaner spray, always wear safety glasses, rubber gloves, and if sensitive to smells or don't want to breathe in the spray, wear a breathing mask.

Take your skillet outside and spray it with the oven cleaner. I use the one with a yellow cap and is a brand name. I think it works better. After you've covered your piece completely, front and back, top and bottom, stick it in a plastic garbage bag and seal it up. Stick the bag in a warm (works better when warmer) place for a few days. Take it out of the bag in a few days and rinse it off.

At this point, you'll be able to see how well it is working on your piece. You may want to do a little scrubbing at this time with a stainless steel scrubby. Remember, never use copper scrubbers or brushes on cast iron. If it's not to your liking for cleanliness, spray it again, and back in the bag, it goes for another day or so. Pull it out and repeat until clean of organic material.

You may be noticing that there is some rust, you can take care of it by soaking the skillet in a 50/50 mixture of vinegar and water. NEVER let the piece soak for more than 30 minutes at a time. Vinegar is very acidic. After a half hour soak, take the piece out and scrub clean. Repeat if necessary.

Once you have removed all the crud and rust from your skillet, you will want to wash it. Yes, I said wash it. Wash it with Dawn dish soap and cold water until no black or rust comes off. You can also use a magic eraser to help this process as well. Remember to squeeze the eraser a lot during use. At this point, you are ready to season or spray with vegetable oil to protect from rust till you can season. Oven cleaner is aerosol lye.

Chicken Corn Fritters

Ingredients

1 can (15-1/4 ounces) whole kernel corn, drained
1 cup finely chopped cooked chicken
1 large egg, lightly beaten
1/2 cup whole milk
2 tablespoons butter, melted
1/2 teaspoon salt
1/8 teaspoon pepper
1-3/4 cups all-purpose flour
1 teaspoon baking powder
Oil for deep-fat frying

Directions

Place corn in a large bowl; lightly crush with a potato masher. Stir in the chicken, egg, milk, butter, salt, and pepper. Combine flour and baking powder; stir into the corn mixture just until combined.
In a deep-fat fryer or skillet, heat 2 in. of oil to 375°. Drop batter by 1/4 cups into oil. Fry for 3 minutes on each side or until golden brown. Drain on paper towels; keep warm.

Removing Rust

One might think that removing rust from something takes a lot of force. This is not true. A vinegar and water mixture will loosen and remove rust. Please do not use power tools or sandblast to remove rust. You can damage the skillet to the point where it won't hold seasoning.

Make a 50/50 water-vinegar mixture and soak your piece in it for 30 minutes at a time. Vinegar is very acidic, this is why it's mixed with water instead of full strength. Seriously, damage to your cast iron can happen from leaving it in there too long. Place it in the mixture and wait 30 minutes and then rinse and scrub till the rust is gone. If still rusty, repeat soaking and scrubbing process till gone.

Corned Beef Hash

Ingredients
1-1/4 pounds potatoes (about 3 medium), cut into 1/2-inch cubes
3 tablespoons butter
3/4 cup finely chopped celery
3/4 pound cooked corned beef, cut into 1/2-inch cubes (about 2-1/2 cups)
4 green onions, chopped
1/4 teaspoon pepper
Dash ground cloves

Directions
Place potatoes in a saucepan; add water to cover. Bring to a boil. Reduce heat; cook, uncovered, just until tender, 6-8 minutes. Drain. In a large skillet, heat butter over medium-high heat. Add celery; cook and stir until crisp-tender, 4-6 minutes. Add potatoes; cook until lightly browned, turning occasionally, 6-8 minutes. Stir in corned beef; cook until heated through, 1-2 minutes. Sprinkle with green onions, pepper, and cloves; cook 1-2 minutes longer. Grandmother served with fried eggs and toast.

Lye Tank

A lye tank is just that. A tank with a lye and water mixture to soak your skillets in till the crud comes off. A lye tank can be very useful. It costs way less than oven cleaner and lasts a lot longer. With this method as well, a small amount of danger exists. You will have a tub of lye that you don't want kids or animals getting into, so make sure it's in a safe place or you can lock it up.

One of the nice things about lye is that you can leave your piece in there indefinitely if you want to. Some people I know have had pieces in there for 6 months or more. Not that it will take that long. That will be determined upon the piece you are cleaning and how bad it is.

What you do is get a heavy-duty plastic container big enough to hold multiple pans at once. Some people use old coolers with latches and fashion a lock for it. Fill it with lye and water mixture at a ratio of 1 pound of lye to 5 gallons of water. Remember to add the lye to the water, not the water to the lye to cut down the risk of splashing on you. Stir it up and start adding the pieces you want to be cleaned.

Some people use a lye tank in conjunction with an electrolysis tank. This does a couple of things for them. First, they will have more pieces of CI ready to season at one time. Second, it takes less time in the E-tank to remove the rest of the crud. Remember, lye does NOT remove rust.

Please use safety equipment, such as rubber gloves, eye protection, and a breathing mask when filling and working with a lye tank!

Electrolysis Tank

This has to be my favorite method of cleaning my cast iron. With an E-tank, it takes most, if not all, of the crud and rust off of the metal. Some crud is very stubborn, and these pieces go into my lye tank for a long soak. However, most pieces can be stripped to bare metal within 12 to 24 hours.

So exactly what is Electrolysis? Electrolysis is a process where electric current is passed through an electrolyte liquid that conducts electricity. This is obtained because the liquid contains ions. An E-tank consists of these parts in order to make it work properly: tank, cathode, anode, electrolyte, manual battery charger.

The negative electrode, called the Cathode, will attract positively charged metal ions. The metal ions collect electrons from the cathode (this is called reduction) and are discharged as metal atoms.

The positive electrode, called the Anode, will attract negatively charged non-metal ions. The non-metal ions lose electrons to the anode and are discharged as non-metal atoms.

Even though it's relatively safe, there is still some danger associated with this method. You will be working with electricity and water so stay alert and don't be distracted. There is also a small amount of hydrogen that is produced from the reaction caused by the operation. A well-ventilated area to run your tank should be used.

The amount of hydrogen is very small but could build up if used in a closed area. That and the fact that you're using a battery charger with potential sparks makes following certain operation procedures a must.

Setting up an E-tank is really very simple. The items you will need are a manual (NOT automatic) battery charger, a plastic container to hold the water solution, a 5-gallon bucket, a storage tote, and a small garbage can. Or a plastic barrel will work. The size you choose depends on you and what you think you'll be cleaning in your tank.

You will need some ferrous metal for your anode(s). You can buy new iron at a metal supplier, Home Depot scrap yard etc. Any ferrous metal will work, but I prefer a stainless-steel anode. It will last a lot longer and does a better job cleaning. I found two sheets of a restaurant dishwasher at the junkyard for mine. They line the insides of my container 360 degrees and are attached by a pair of old jumper cables to achieve contact with each other.

You will also need a manual battery charger: My charger is a commercial roll around charger and I use it on the 12-volt, 40-amp setting. For pans showing lots of rust and crud, it will normally take about 12 hours or so to clean. For your container: I recommend you use one that is large enough to hold the largest piece of cast iron you think you will ever clean. My tank is a 35-gallon plastic heavy duty garbage can.

The solution: you make an electrolyte solution by mixing sodium carbonate with water at the rate of 1/2 cup sodium carbonate to every 5 gallons of water. Sodium Carbonate can be found as Arm & Hammer Super Washing Soda at most grocery and hardware stores like Ace. It can also be found at swimming pool supply stores as it is used in swimming pools to increase the Ph of the water which keeps the water clear. Make sure to mix the solution 5 gallons at a time to be sure it is mixed thoroughly.

Okay... after you have your tank made you need to place your anode(s) in the tank. I recommend the largest flat sheets you can find or afford. Electrolysis works on "line-of-sight" so the more surface area you have the more action you will have for cleaning.

Since the anode is sacrificial, meaning it is going to erode as it is used, then the thicker the metal the better. Cookie sheets and baking pans will work but will get "eaten up" fairly quickly. I suggest 1/8" to 1/4" material for a longer life for your anodes. Stainless steel will last much longer and be easier to clean. As you use your E-tank the anodes will corrode with rust and crud from your pans so you will have to remove them for cleaning occasionally. Keep that in mind when placing them for easy removal and re-installing them.

I also suggest placing your anode(s) so that you have an anode on each side of the pan you are cleaning, suspending the pan down from a crossbar on top of your tank so the pan hangs in between the anodes as close as possible but never touching the pan to the anode. If using anodes on each side of the pan you will need to securely attach one anode to the other by means of a wire, strap, or another method. Just make sure you have a good solid tight connection by using bolts, washers, and nuts to fasten tightly.

Now your tank is ready to be filled and place your pan. As mentioned above the best way (not the only way) is to suspend your pan down between your anodes. I use a short piece of dog chain with "S" hooks. One through the pan's handle for instance and the other "S" hook hooked over a cross rod on top of my tank and adjust the chain so the pan hangs freely, not touching the tank bottom.

Don't use the suspension chain to hook your battery lead to as there are too many loose links to interrupt the current. Use a small C clamp to clamp your negative wire to your pan, making sure the connection spot is free of rust and crud so you have direct contact with the metal. Too much crud or rust can act as an insulator blocking the current from the charger. You can also attach the negative lead wire through the handle hole by using some flat washers, bolt, and nut to get a good tight connection.

After you have everything set up, take your RED Positive lead from the charger and connect it to an anode. Take the BLACK negative lead from the charger and connect it to the wire that goes directly to the pan. Note: you can also connect the negative battery lead directly on the pan down in the water but if you do a lot of pans it will eventually rust and corrode the clamp spring and it will break. After you have connected the battery leads and double checked to make sure your connections are tight, and your pan is not touching the anodes, then you can plug in the battery charger and turn it on.

In a few seconds, you should see small bubbles coming from the pan. Congratulations! Your electrolysis tank is working. If you don't see bubbles then make sure the outlet that your charger is plugged into is working, then recheck your connections. Always turn off your charger or unplug it when checking your connections or removing your battery leads. That's all there is to it. Joining Electrolysis Tank Builders on Facebook can help you with any additional questions on E-tanks.

Seasoning Cast Iron

Many different ideas on seasoning cast iron are out there. From the type of oil to use to the temperature you season at, and for how long, are all debatable. The process of seasoning puts a coat on your skillet to protect it from rust. Some believe that the seasoning is what makes it stick free. This is untrue.

When the seasoning process occurs, the oil you have put on the skillet reaches and exceeds the smoke point level and all the molecules in the oil line up and create a bond. This is called polymerization. This is what gives the cast iron that nice black look and protects it.

Different oils are going to give you different results. Some will make the iron a dark black and others will turn it a bronze. No matter the color it will still be protected if this process is followed. Different oils have higher or lower smoke points. Knowing what the smoke point of the oil you are using will help you get the right seasoning on your skillet. Smoke point chart is at the end of the book in the appendix.

Whichever oil you choose, be sure to season at a temperature that is at least 100°F above the smoke point of that oil. I use Crisco shortening for my seasoning, which has a smoke point of 350°F, and I season at 475°F. I feel that seasoning at a temperature that you will most likely never cook at will ensure that the seasoning is ready for any temp you throw at it. If you don't at least reach the smoke point of your oil, your skillet will come out all sticky and that is NOT what you want. Your piece of cast iron should be dry to the touch when it is properly seasoned.

The process I'm about to lay out to you is the way I season my iron. It may not be the best way or a way you have heard of, but it's the best one I've found that works for me. I will walk you through my seasoning technique step by step, hopefully not leaving you to ask more questions than when we started.

The first thing I do when starting to season cast iron is I make sure that I have everything that I'm going to need close and ready. These things include, but are not limited to, a thick piece of cardboard to sit a hot skillet on, hot pads, paper towels, basting brush, Crisco, and clean dry cotton towels. All of these items are dedicated to seasoning and are used for nothing else. The cotton towels will never be usable for any other job since it will be oil soaked until washed and then will still smell like oil.

Take your clean, down-to-bare-metal skillet and put it in the oven right side up with the door slightly open at 200°F for 15 minutes. After your skillet has warmed to 200, take it out and set it on cardboard using a hot pad. Using folded up paper towels (the thicker the better for burnt fingers), take a small amount of Crisco and carefully wipe it on the skillet, everywhere. Top, bottom, sides, and handle.

Once you have it completely covered in oil, take some wadded-up paper towels and wipe off as much of the oil as you can. Remember, it's hot! When you think you have it dry, take one of your cotton towels (I use old kitchen hand towels) and wipe it dry again. Then, take your other cotton towel and wipe it one more time. This is a very, very important part of the process. You may be thinking, what is he talking about? I'm not wiping anything off. It's totally dry! Well, it's not and this will make it so that it doesn't pool and be blotchy or spotty.

Ok, now we have it wiped off as dry as we can and are going to stick it in the oven UPSIDE DOWN on the rack. This is to make sure no oil pools on the cooking surface. You may want to put some aluminum foil on the bottom rack in case some oil drips. If we wiped it dry, it shouldn't. Now close the door all the way and increase temp to 475°F. About 10 minutes later, I remove it and wipe one more time with the last towel I used and put back in face down and bake for at least one hour. Turn oven off and let cool naturally.

Guess what? You just seasoned a skillet! Congratulations!! You're all done! Well... not really. You do have a seasoning on your skillet and it will protect it from rust for a period of time, but if you don't use it and build up the seasoning, it will eventually start rusting again. Don't worry, I'm going to help you get a little farther along a little more quickly than using it daily. Don't get me wrong, there is no better way to season a skillet than to use it, but we're going to give it a little boost.

A couple of my daily users have had that title for about a year now and have had many pounds of bacon and potatoes fried in them. They are a slick jet black and have the most beautiful seasoning on them. They started out being seasoned the same way we discussed here, except for one thing. When I told you to turn the oven off and let it cool, don't. Instead, be very careful and take the skillet out and reapply some Crisco and wipe it off, in the same manner, discussed earlier and bake for another hour. Remember, that skillet is HOT, 475°F. Every time you do this, you add another layer of seasoning on your skillet.

I usually do about four or five rounds of seasoning on a freshly stripped skillet. There is no need to do this for cooking reasons, but I like my cast iron to look a dark black faster, so this is what I do. Whatever you choose to do, just remember that you can always fix it if it gets messed up. It's time to start cooking with it. What are you going to cook first?

In the next section we will talk about breaking in your new/new to you skillet.

Cooking and Care

Here we are, we have our new or recently restored skillet and we're ready to cook. Not, so fast. There are a few things I would recommend you do to help you enjoy using your skillet more. Seeing as your skillet only has a relatively light seasoning, you will want to refrain from cooking certain foods to start with. Until your seasoning is well established you should steer away from acidic foods. These will eat away at your seasoning. The skillets I mentioned earlier, my daily users, are so nicely seasoned I wouldn't fear cooking anything in them now.

So, what should you cook first? I recommend starting with frying some cubed potatoes. Cube up some potatoes and toss them in some olive oil, making sure they are completely covered and add whatever seasonings you want. Warm your pan on a low heat. On my glass top stove, I set my temp at 2 to 3 on the dial. When the skillet is warm, add potatoes and start frying while moving them around continuously for a few minutes, then every so often after that. When they are nicely browned you can eat them or throw them away, your choice. Sometimes the first thing cooked in a new pan isn't always the best tasting, don't know why, just is.

At this point you should already notice a difference in the way your skillet is starting to look.

Frying bacon and potatoes will build your seasoning about as fast as anything will. If your skillet has a lid or you have one that will fit it, try popping some popcorn using that bacon grease you saved. We save all our bacon grease and use it all the time for a variety of things. Speaking of bacon, when frying bacon in cast iron, if the skillet is really hot and you put the bacon in the skillet, it's going to stick. Using some of that saved bacon grease in the skillet while it's warming up will help that.

One of the biggest mistakes people make when first starting out cooking on cast iron is have their heat way too high. One of the first things that I learned about CI cooking was "Low and Slow". There is a lot of wisdom in this statement, low heat and slow cooking will make you a happier CI cook. Every range has its own identity, you will have to play with your temperature dial for a while until you find the sweet spot. There are times when you will want more heat, such as when deep frying or searing a steak.

Another common mistake is trying to turn or flip your food too early. If you try and turn it too early, your food is going to stick. Instead, wait for the item to release itself from the skillet, then turn. You can sometimes physically see the steak or eggs release themselves from the pan. Adding more oil to keep food from sticking is only going to give you greasier food. Sure it might not stick, but now you have soggy hash browns and for me, that's not a good thing.

Never get mad at your seasoning for your food sticking. It's not its fault. In reality, you don't even need seasoning to cook on CI. Like I said earlier, seasoning is there to protect the skillet from rusting, not to make it stick free. I have seen videos of eggs being cooked on a bare metal skillet and when done, the egg slid right of without using any utensils. It's all about temperature and patience.

Wondering what kind of recipes you can make in your CI? The answer, ANYTHING! Remember, it is just a cooking pan like any other you have ever used. It just gets hotter and cooks more evenly. So just take it slow and experiment with it. Soon you'll be like me and wonder how you ever got along without your CI!

I told you I was only going to have a small section on cooking and this is true. I can only give you the few hints I have learned that I wish I knew at the beginning. Food sticking seems to be most people's problem when cooking with CI. It is definitely something that takes a little time and practice using. It is just that much more different than your stainless-steel pan is.

Let's talk about the care of your cast iron. This is where I hear people saying it's too hard to care for, so I don't use it. Well, I'm here to tell you, that's not true. As with anything of value to you, you are going to take a little extra care of it to keep it looking good and last longer. Your CI should be no different. Let's go over a few of the myths and realities of CI care.

Myths. There are a ton of them out there about cast iron. While some of them are completely out there, others held some truth at one point in time. I already talked about the myth of seasoning being the reason food doesn't stick, so I'll not go on about that anymore. Here's one, "Don't wash your CI with soap!". This is one that used to be true but doesn't hold up today.

When the people of the 1800s and early 1900s cleaned their cast iron they didn't want to use soap, because it was made with lye. We learned earlier that lye is what we use to strip our CI, so it's understandable that the saying was used. In today's time, we don't have this worry since our soap is not lye based. I would suggest using a soft style of soap when cleaning.

Never put your CI in the dishwasher. This is good advice. The temperature of the water and the soap together can harm your seasoning and expose the metal to rust. Hand cleaning your CI is the best way and if you've seasoned and cooked properly with it, it should wipe clean with just a paper towel.

Another myth is that you shouldn't boil water in your CI. At times, this is true. When your cast iron is newly seasoned, boiling water in it can cause the seasoning to flake off. Once you have a really established seasoning the boiling water will be less invasive.

One thing you definitely don't want to do is put cold water in a hot skillet. This can result in the skillet cracking or exploding right in front of you. This could be very dangerous and should be thought of often. Some of the ingredients you use may be cold, so be careful. Likewise, never put the hot skillet in cold water.

My system of cleaning my cast iron after cooking depends a lot on what I have just made. If I've just made bacon, most of the time I can just wipe it out and it's good to go the next time. But sometimes some particles will stick, no problem. I let the skillet cool down and the put it in the sink and run hot water over it while scrubbing with a nylon cleaning brush. This is usually enough to get it clean.

Sometimes you'll end up with food that is really stuck on. If the above method doesn't do the trick, go ahead and wash it with soap and water. It's ok! Just make sure you rinse it well. There are products on the market made just for cleaning cast iron, but I have never seen a need for them. In extreme cases, you can pour a little hot water in a warm skillet and bring to boil while scraping the bottom at the same time.

After my cast iron is clean and still warm from washing, I take a little Crisco and wipe the cooking surface with it. Then, take a clean paper towel and wipe it dry and put away till next time.

No matter how you get your CI clean, keep in mind, you can always restore it if you do screw it up!

Apple Pie

Ingredients
2-1/2 cups all-purpose flour
1/2 teaspoon salt
1-1/4 cups cold lard
6 to 8 tablespoons cold milk

FILLING:
2-1/2 cups sugar
1 teaspoon ground cinnamon
1/2 teaspoon ground ginger
9 cups thinly sliced peeled tart apples (about 9 medium)
1 tablespoon bourbon, optional
2 tablespoons all-purpose flour
Dash salt
3 tablespoons cold butter, cubed

TOPPING:
1 tablespoon milk
2 teaspoons coarse sugar

Directions
In a large bowl, mix flour and salt; cut in lard until crumbly. Gradually add milk, tossing with a fork until dough holds together when pressed. Divide dough in

half. Shape each into a disk; wrap in plastic. Refrigerate 1 hour or overnight.

For filling, in a large bowl, mix sugar, cinnamon, and ginger. Add apples and toss to coat. Cover; let stand 1 hour to allow apples to release juices, stirring occasionally.

Drain apples, reserving syrup. Place syrup and, if desired, bourbon in a small saucepan; bring to a boil. Reduce heat; simmer, uncovered, 20-25 minutes or until mixture thickens slightly and turns a medium amber color. Remove from heat; cool completely.

Preheat oven to 400°. Toss drained apples with flour and salt. On a lightly floured surface, roll one half of dough to a 1/8-in.-thick circle; transfer to a 10-in. cast-iron skillet. Trim pastry even with rim. Add apple mixture. Pour cooled syrup over top; dot with butter.

Roll remaining dough to a 1/8-in.-thick circle. Place over filling. Trim, seal and flute edge. Cut slits in top. Brush milk over pastry; sprinkle with coarse sugar. Place on a foil-lined baking sheet. Bake 20 minutes.

Reduce oven setting to 350°. Bake 45-55 minutes longer or until crust is golden brown and filling is bubbly. Cool on a wire rack.

Final Thoughts

I am truly hoping that the information in this book helps at least one person. If it does, it will be worth every minute I spent writing this. I really enjoyed writing this book, it was such a relief to finally be able to put all of this down on paper. I've had this stuff rattling around in my brain for years and now it's out. I don't expect this book to be used as a field guide, I wrote it to help anyone that is new to cast iron get a helpful start on their journey into the cast iron world.

All the information in this book was obtained by me through online research, discussions with Cast Iron collectors, and my own trial and errors. All dates stated in here are to be used as a guideline and not exact dates. They are close but may not be 100% accurate due to lost or damaged foundry records.

A special thanks to Windy A. Ford for her family recipes and Jamie Grigg and Dru Humphrey for their incredible knowledge. I really appreciate your help!

        I hope you enjoy your Cast Iron Journey,
                Jim Anderson

Additional help and information on all subjects covered here can be found on Facebook at these groups.

Sharing Cast Iron Only
https://www.facebook.com/groups/1084557164997333/

Electrolysis Tank Builders
https://www.facebook.com/groups/ElectrolysisTanks/

Resources:

N. (s.d.). Evolution of the Wagner Trademark. Accessed on 2/20/2019 through http://www.castironcollector.com/wagnertm.php

Lodge Cast Iron. (March 8, 2017). The Story Of Our Founder Joseph Lodge. Accessed on 2/21/2019 through http://www.lodgemfg.com/about

N. (s.d.). Vollrath Manufacturing Company. Accessed on 2/22/2019 through http://www.castironcollector.com/vollrath.php

N. (s.d.). Evolution of the Griswold Trademark. Accessed on 2/19/2019 through http://www.castironcollector.com/griswoldtm.php

N. (s.d.). Birmingham Stove and Range Co.. Accessed on 2/17/2019 through www.castironcollector.com/birmingham.php

Glossary

CI- Cast Iron

Knock offs- A skillet that was made off the pattern of another

Spinners- A skillet that bows down and spins

Foundry- Building where the cast iron is poured

Heat Ring- Raised ring around the bottom of skillet

Milled- Technique used to make the cooking surface smooth

Grooved- Refers to skillet handles that have a scooped out bottom

Smooth Bottom- Skillet bottom without heat ring

Notch- A cut out in the heat ring on a skillet

Hammered- Technique to make skillet sides look hammered (dented)

Logo- Brand name or design on the bottom of skillet

LBL- Large Block Logo

SBL- Small Block Logo

Makers Mark- Small mark or letter on skillet bottom

Incised- Letter or numbers cut into the surface

Raised- Letter or numbers that are raised above the surface

Polymerization- The process that makes molecules form a polymer chain in oils to protect your skillet

Seasoning- The coating put on a skillet to protect it

Appendix

Cooking Oils/Fats	Smoke Point °C	Smoke Point °F
Flaxseed Oil	107	225
Unrefined Safflower Oil	107	225
Unrefined Sunflower Oil	107	225
Unrefined Corn Oil	160	320
Unrefined High Oleic Sunflower Oil	160	320
Extra Virgin Olive Oil	160	320
Unrefined Peanut Oil	160	320
Semi-refined Safflower Oil	160	320
Unrefined Soy Oil	160	320

Unrefined Walnut Oil	160	320
Hemp Seed Oil	165	330
Butter	177	350
Semi-refined Canola Oil	177	350
Coconut Oil	177	350
Unrefined Sesame Oil	177	350
Semi-refined Soy Oil	177	350
Vegetable Shortening	182	360
Lard	182	370
Macadamia Nut Oil	199	390
Canola Oil	200	400
Refined Canola Oil	204	400
Semi-refined Walnut Oil	204	400

High-Quality Extra Virgin Olive Oil	207	405
Sesame Oil	210	410
Cottonseed Oil	216	420
Grapeseed Oil	216	420
Virgin Olive Oil	216	420
Almond Oil	216	420
Hazelnut Oil	221	430
Peanut Oil	227	440
Sunflower Oil	227	440
Refined Corn Oil	232	450
Palm Oil	232	450
Palm Kernel Oil	232	450
Refined High Sunflower Oil	232	450

Refined Peanut Oil	232	450
Semi-refined Sesame Oil	232	450
Refined Soy Oil	232	450
Semi-refined Sunflower Oil	232	450
Olive Pomace Oil	238	460
Extra Light Olive Oil	242	468
Ghee (Clarified Butter)	252	485
Rice Bran Oil	254	490
Refined Safflower Oil	266	510
Avocado Oil	271	520

Personal Notes

Made in the USA
Lexington, KY
23 October 2019